THE JOY OF
OYSTERS

DON QUINN

To
Diane
Best wishes

Typeset by Green Square Design
www.greensquare.me

Printed by AutoPrint
www.autoprint.co.uk

A catalogue record for this book
is available from the British Library.

The Author makes no representation, express or implied, with regard to the accuracy of the information contained in this book and cannot accept any legal responsibility for any errors or omissions that may take place.

The views and opinions expressed in this book are exclusively those of the Author for which they accept full responsibility.

This book is printed on FSC (Forest Stewardship Council) certified paper. FSC-certified forests are managed in ways that safeguard long-term timber supplies, whilst protecting the environment and lives of forest-dependent peoples.

CONTENTS

INTRODUCTION
By The Author

I can remember my father buying one opened oyster in Blackpool sometime in the 1950's, at a window in Roberts' Oyster Rooms. Still open today and still selling oysters.

We all watched as our brave warrior essayed upon this delicacy. We gasped as he glugged it down. We waited in high tension for the reaction. 'Marvellous' our hero said, and strode off toward the pier with us all in tow.

My intrepid Dad bought a tin of ravioli in a shop in Leeds in the 1950s. He had aquired a taste for Italian food during WW2 when he was stationed by the army in Italy. It was considered very adventerous if not downright dangerous to eat 'foreign' food. We had one of the little savoury parcels each!

I suppose my dad's food adventures must have created a bit of an interest in food in general and oysters in particular for me, but it was many years before I tried an oyster myself. I graduated from cockles (which I still love both fresh and pickled), munched my way through prawns, shrimps, crabs and even lobster before I finally arrived at oysters.

Some twenty years after my dad's Blackpool oyster, me and my wife moved to Colchester – famous for its oysters. We had temporary digs with ex mayor of the town Len Woodrow. He told me if I was going to live in Colchester I should eat oysters. So I did.

I went to a shack on Mersea Island with a chum, Paul St Amour. The proprietor of the now defunct shack seemed to be somewhat worse for wear, an impression added to by the numerous empty wine bottles! I bought a dozen open oysters and loved them immediately.

Some years later I struck up a friendship with Richard Haward and his wife Heather. Richard fishes for oysters and is often on television and in the media. He taught me lots about oysters. With the rest of their family they run the world famous 'The Company Shed' on Mersea Island. A wonderful and atmospheric place to eat oysters and lots of other seafood.

> *Oysters are the most tender and delicate of all seafoods. The stay in bed all day and night. They never work or take exercise, are stupendous drinkers, and wait for their meals to come to them.*

Hector Bolitho, The Glorious Oyster (1929)

There are plenty of literary and poetic references to oysters, some of which I have included in this book. I did a gig with legendary punk poet Dr John Cooper Clarke in a circus 'big top' in the middle of Colchester's famous Castle Park. Ten minutes before I went on stage to announce the big man himself I was challenged to create and deliver a poem. This is it. Tis a poor thing but tis mine own:

> *I am a juicy oyster. I live in the cold sea.*
> *I am an hermaphrodite, that's both he and she.*
> *What can a lonely oyster do, sitting on a rocky shelf.*
> *But sit beneath the waves all day having sex with myself.*
> *Full of fun and frolics, happy as can be.*
> *Till some rotten sod pulled me out and ate me for his tea!*

Don Quinn

I won the bet and got a laugh.

In 2003 I created the Colchester Food and Drink Festival which takes place on the last weekend of June every year. We found lots of people wanted to buy our oysters and even more wanted to know more about this amazing mollusc. For the first time in many years in Colchester we had on sale a cooked oyster product, a steak and oyster pie. This went down very well indeed with the local beer and an idea was born.

In 2009, with an amazing character called Terry Croucher, we established the Colchester Oyster Festival on the first Saturday of September. In between Terry and I occasionally sold oysters on markets and organize food and drink festivals for Food and Drink Festivals UK Ltd. and Snake in the Grass Events.

The Oyster Festival was established to promote Colchester and its top quality oysters. Our aim is for it to be an inclusive event – involving everyone.

Oysters are the only food you will eat whilst it is still alive!

I prefer my oysters fried. That way I know my oyster's died.

Roy Blount, Jr.

We often had people ask 'can you cook oysters?'. Some because they were not too sure about eating a live animal, feelings shared by Roy Blount (above) and Woody Allen:

I will not eat oysters. I want my food dead – not sick, not wounded – dead.

The answer was, of course, yes you can cook (and therefore kill) oysters, but the only recipes I knew were 'Angels on Horseback' and steak pie with oysters.

So I talked to chefs I knew and got stuck into research. With plenty of oysters supplied uncomplainingly by my friend Richard Haward I experimented with lots of different recipes I had found. A wonderful chef called Paul Borman helped. At one stage he even used a motorized bong to delicately smoke an oyster using dried porcini mushroom. What he does with the bong in his own time is his business.

The results of all this work can be found in the recipe section.

Still-Life with Oysters by Alexander Adriaenssen, C.1630

early man attempts to open oysters

CHAPTER 1

A BIT OF OYSTER HISTORY

Humankind has eaten oysters since the dawn of time. Palaeontologists trace the existence of oysters back to at least the Triassic (about 248 to 213 million years ago).

They have grown from simple protein rich stomach filler eaten by the poorest of people to a gastronomic delicacy for the rich. Now the wheel has turned and oysters are once again affordable for a wide range of people. Will they ever become as plentiful as when poor Medieval London Apprentices complained that they were being fed too many oysters? I think not, but they are gradually becoming more and more popular as they become more economically available.

Many anthropologists believe that there were a number of compelling reasons for Stone Age people to settle near the sea shore, the home of the oyster. Collecting oysters and other shellfish was far more convenient and a lot less dangerous than hunting wild game; oysters are sitting ducks, as they can't run away; while hunting was generally reserved only for the men, the entire family including the women folk, and the children, could forage for shellfish throughout the year. Thus allowing men to say 'You go out today dear I seem to have hurt my leg drinking with Tharg'.

Oysters are very unsatisfactory food for the labouring men, but will do for the sedentary, and for a supper to sleep on.

Albert J. Bellows

It was a bold man that first ate on oyster.

Jonathan Swift

It certainly was a brave person who first ate an oyster, or so they say. Frankly I suspect it was a very hungry person who first ate an oyster. They take some opening without a knife.

Bashing them with one slippery stone against another can have painful side effects which is where the saying, 'Tharg has a face like a blind oyster opener's thumb' might have emerged.

The man had a sure palate cover'd o'er
With brass or steel, that on the rocky shore
First broke the oozy oyster's pearly coat
And risqu'd the living morsel down his throat

John Gaye

Indeed it may well be that after mankind had smashed his way into this well armoured mollusc the bright little fellow (actually my money is on a woman) hit on a plan. If you bung oysters into the embers of your fire they open all by themselves. No need to bash them with a rock and then have to pick the squelchy parts from the hard bits. Give the oysters a minute or two at regulo medium embers and bingo. Not only open but damn tasty and hot.

Thus could the cooking of oysters have begun, and eating them cooked was probably more normal than eating them raw until the knife was invented.

Stone Age man ultimately loved oysters. The discoveries of huge prehistoric shell middens in many coastal regions of the world prove that oysters have been part of mankind's diet for many thousands of years. Permanent settlements of prehistoric man existed 6,000 years ago along the Baltic Sea in northern Europe. Their kitchen middens reveal lots of oyster shells. The same holds true for the kitchen middens of the coastal Indians of North America 4,000 years ago. In contrast to the European tribes, the North American Indians were already cooking their oysters. There's even talk of a 'prehistoric oyster stew'.

It was the Romans who helped to popularize oysters in England, and established their cultivation in my hometown of Colchester. They were one of the first in history to produce cultivated oysters. They loved raw oysters but they also loved them cooked. I have included a Roman recipe in the recipe section, which I have adapted slightly for practical reasons so you can try it for yourself.

The rich waters off Camulodunum, or as we know it, Colchester, were particularly suitable to the raising of this most delicious mollusc. And still produce wonderful oysters today.

Poor Britons, there is some good in them after all – they produced an oyster.

Roman historian, when the Roman invaders discovered the natural oyster beds in East Anglia.

Before the Romans arrived in Britain in AD 43, Britons thought of shellfish as something you ate only if you had to. Fish or meat was preferred. However, the Romans brought with them an enthusiasm for eating seafood of all kinds – from jellyfish to rotten fish gut sauce. As soon as the Roman invasion was over and traders and civilians began to arrive, a demand quickly built up for all kinds of fish and shellfish. The shells of oysters have been found extensively on the sites of Roman villas, towns (including Colchester), and forts at least as far north as Hadrian's Wall, not only near the coast but also at great distances from the sea, having been presumably transported alive in water tanks.

Oysters were Britain's glory. They were marketed widely within the country, and were even sent as far as Rome itself.

After the Romans left oysters still flourished and indeed in the Anglo Saxon period Debby Banham in her book on Anglo Saxon cookery likens them to 'tapas'. She points out that in this period that oysters were plentiful and available in places which sold wine and ale. Part of the attraction of oysters is that the church decreed days when meat must not be eaten, such as Lent, but oysters being designated fish were allowed. This passage from the late Anglo Saxon period 'Seasons for Fasting' gives us a flavour of the times.

> *But I can say, tearful with sorrows, how the priests make trouble again.*
> *Every day, anger the Lord and maliciously lead astray every one of the people who is willing to follow them.*
> *First thing in the morning they sing mass, and consumed by thirst, after to the tapster they haul through the streets.*
> *Look! They deceitfully start lying and keep egging on the tapster, say that without sin he can give them oysters to eat and noble wine.*

Richard I in 1189 granted the Borough of Colchester a charter giving it control of the fishery. Over the next 800 years and more this has created major amounts of cash for the council. The oyster is now celebrated in the annual Oyster Festival held in Lower Castle Park on the first Saturday in September. If you are reading this you should go to the Festival!

Viking combined oyster opening service and complaints department!

Well before the Norman Conquest in the 11th century, the old Roman practice of transporting shellfish inland had been revived, and by the 1400s the oyster was a popular foodstuff for rich and poor alike, sometimes cooked in its own juices with a little ale and pepper.

In the 15th century even rent was paid in oysters, and dues to the monastery:

> *In 1411 one Nicholas Diford, a copyholder of Meonstoke, came to the audit with 100 oysters in payment of his quit rent. These doubtless came from Hamble, which was formerly in high repute for its oysters. The prior of Hamble used to render 20,000 oysters at mid-Lent to the monks of St. Swithun as an acknowledgment for*

an annual corrody of six gowns, six pairs of shoes, six pairs of boots,
together with twenty-one loaves and forty-two flagons of ale weekly,
which he and his brethren received from that monastery.

A History of the County of Hampshire

The English king Henry IV (1367–1413) supposedly downed 400 oysters in one sitting – purely as an appetizer.

During the Middle Ages, it was generally known that the oyster 'exciteth Venus'.

Throughout the medieval period, the church imposed a very large number of 'fish days', where the meat of animals and birds could not be eaten. Lent and all Fridays and Saturdays were kept as fish days until the late Middle Ages, and Wednesdays were also observed until the early 15th century. Oysters were included in the list of permitted foods so improving their popularity.

Lots of methods of cooking oysters started to appear and flourished from the 17th century onwards. Fowls of all kinds were stuffed with or cooked alongside oysters. Oyster sauce became common and sausages were created with oysters and other meats.

Scotland too had an oyster history in the Firth of Forth, which it defended fiercely. When Essex boatmen approached, they were bombarded with stones. Where today a sign reads not to eat fish caught in the waters, in the late 1800s as many as 30 million oysters were taken a year.

The oyster girl with her creel was a familiar sight doing her rounds of the tenements. Some of this culture was caught in song, the oyster humbled to just two letters in the dialect as o'u:

At night round the ingle sae canty are we,
The oyster lass brings her treat frae the sea;
Wi music and sang, as time passes by,
We hear in the distance the creel-lassie's cry.

Caller o'u! Caller o'u! Caller o'u!
Frae the Forth. Caller o'u! Caller o'u

Oysters were still eaten on their own, of course, as an hors d'oeuvre or in the main meal, and from the 17th century they were routinely pickled for transport to inland towns or for long voyages. Small fresh oysters were eaten raw; large ones were stewed with herbs and spices, or were roasted or baked in pies.

During the 18th century, green oysters became popular. In Essex around Mersea and the rivers Crouch and Roach, oysters developed green beards of harmless algae in September. Local salesmen collected them and put them into pits dug in the saltmarshes for six to eight weeks, turning them a deep dark green, and they were much admired in London.

In 1808 a UK law was passed making theft of oysters punishable by transportation or prison.

Oysters continued in popularity into Victorian times. Fresh and live oysters when there was an 'r' in the month and pickled oysters all year were a regular food of the poor in London and other towns. As Dickens' Sam Weller remarks, 'Poverty and oysters always seem to go together'.

There was even a Victorian underground magazine of erotica, published in the 1880's, called *The Oyster*, and devoted to more heterosexual material than its predecessor, *The Pearl*. So it was no small wonder that the poor country girls, the oysterwenches who stalked the streets of the growing cities, hawking their wares, were often regarded as prostitutes.

Charles Dickens wrote fondly of a rogue called Dando. A real life figure who died of cholera in Brixton prison in 1832. His exploits emphasized how ubiquitous oysters and oyster mongers were in London and Kent.

Oysters were Dando's weakness. They had become a staple diet of the 19th century poor, brought up the Thames in barges from the beds in Essex, offloaded at Billingsgate and taken away in their barrel loads to be hawked around London, often on street stalls from where they were eaten straight from the shell. Dando was reputed to have consumed thirty dozen large ones in a single sitting with a proportionate amount of bread and brandy.

The problem was that he never paid. Dando would go into an oyster seller, eat and drink his fill and then with great aplomb announce that he had no money and leave. He was frequently imprisoned but always, on release, went straight out and had a good free feed of oysters. On the evening of his release from one spell in Brixton he walked straight into a shop and devoured thirteen dozen washed down with five bottles of ginger-beer. He took the latter as he was 'troubled with wind in his stomach'. But once again his bill went unpaid.

> One day he walk'd up to an oyster stall,
> To punish the natives, large and small;
> Just thirty dozen he managed to bite,
> With ten penny loaves – what an appetite!
> But when he had done, without saying good day,
> He bolted off, scot free, away;
> He savag'd the oysters, and left the shell –
> Dando, the bouncing seedy swell.

The Life and Death of Dando, The Celebrated Oyster Glutton (Street Ballad)

> ...oysters are the only food that never causes indigestion. Indeed, a man would have to eat sixteen dozen of these acephalous molluscs in order to gain the 315 grammes of nitrogen he requires daily.

Jules Verne, Twenty Thousand Leagues Under the Sea (1870)

Every year, on the first Friday in September, a ceremony is held in the oyster bed waters off Mersea Island, Colchester, to celebrate the bounty there, and to mark the council's claim. And it is a claim worth staking, given that the Colchester native oyster, Ostrea edulis, is famous all over the world.

The Chief Executive reads an original proclamation, which originates from 1256. The flowery language embellishes the simple claim to the fishery rights. The Mayor, or a helper, dredges 'the first oyster', which the mayor eats. The loyal toast is drunk in gin, with a piece of gingerbread to go with it. Colchester was once a major gin producer. Afterwards there is a lunch with more gin followed by wine. Some Councillors get quite merry and suddenly become best friends with people they have been savagely attacking in Town Hall speeches just a few days before. Don't worry – as the hangovers wear off hostilities resume. But it is a great tradition and lots of fun.

Chapter 2

First Open
Your Oyster

Although Mrs Beeton never actually said it, she is famously quoted as starting one of her recipes with the words 'First catch your hare'.

Well in the case of the oyster the best thing to do by far is to buy them directly from the fishery or a reputable fishmonger. Buying oysters online is a great method and they travel remarkably well. After all the Romans transported them from Colchester to Rome 2,000 years ago.

This book is dedicated to cooking and eating both raw and cooked oysters.

Right at the beginning of this chapter let me state that Colchester natives, Ostrea edulis, should never be cooked. No never, not ever. They are far too beautiful and magnificently complex in their flavour and texture to cook. So don't do it.

Essentially there are two main types of oysters available in the UK and many other parts of the world. These are the *native* oyster and the *gigas* or *pacific* oyster. Natives are the ones you buy when there is an 'r' in the month and gigas all year around.

Natives are the most sought after and in my strong opinion should not be messed around with – simply eaten unadorned. If you can't get natives gigas are also great raw but really good for cooking and quite a bit cheaper.

When you buy oysters today in the UK they have a little piece of paper which accompanies them stating that 'These animals must be alive'. They are almost certainly the only food you will ever eat which is still alive as it courses down your gullet. Don't worry it has no nervous system at all so it doesn't feel a thing.

An oyster
is a fish
built like a nut.

Anon

Once you have your oysters you need to breach the shell fortress surrounding this tasty little mollusc.

When we sold oysters on a market we had a regular lady customer who hurled the oysters onto a tile floor. This is not a recommended technique.

It is really important to use a proper oyster knife as anything else is frankly dangerous. So buy one now – a cheap one with a plastic handle will do. You can also buy it with a cheap moulded holder, which can be useful, as a set.

For online help with 'opening oysters', use Google to find a wealth of videos and other links. Some are excellent. However here are the basics:

- Check the oyster to see if the shell is tightly closed, which is an indicator that the oyster is alive. If the shell is slightly open tap it with the knife. If it closes, fine it is alive. If it remains open its dead – get rid of it.

- Hold the oyster under cool running water with one hand while gently scrubbing the shell with a scrubbing brush in the other hand. Rinse the shell to remove any sand or grit that may have been on the exterior. Set the oyster aside.

- Pick up the oyster and hold it in one hand with the smaller half of the hinged shell facing up. The oyster meat and juices are in the larger, lower half of the shell. Hold it very firmly on a stable surface. A chopping board on a work surface is good.

- Slide the tip of the oyster knife into the hinge or lip (the pointed end) of the oyster shell. You may, when you are learning, need some force so be very careful.

- This is the portion of the shell that will separate and allow you to access the oyster meat. Once in slide the oyster knife across the lip of the shell until the knife reaches the other side of the shell. Keep the oyster level – this helps avoid spilling the liquid from inside the shell.

- Pry the top half of the shell from the bottom half taking care not to spill the liquid inside the oyster. The shells will not completely separate at this point.

- Cut the muscle that attaches the top half of the oyster shell to the bottom half with the oyster knife. Remove and discard the top half of the shell. Keep the bottom half of the oyster shell level.

- Slide the oyster knife under the meat to loosen it from the shell. Wipe away any grit or sand on the meat with your fingers. The oyster is now ready for eating.

Right now you have learnt the only real hard bit of dealing with oysters.

Give yourself a pat on the back.

The Birth of Venus by Sandro Botticelli, 1486

CHAPTER 3

ARE YOU AN
OYSTER VIRGIN?

I like to eat an uncooked oyster.
Nothing's slicker, nothing's moister.
Nothing's easier on your gorge
Within your mouth is always best.
For if your mind dwells on an oyster. . .
Nothing's slicker. Nothing's moister.

Song to Oysters

If you are an oyster virgin eat one now. No fuss, no sauce or pepper just a pure naked oyster, hopefully with some liquor. Just tilt the shell on your lip until the oyster and liquor slip into your mouth. I suggest you chew. Others will suggest you swallow straight down. Both are right – it will become your choice, over time, which method you prefer.

Either way your first sensation will be a taste of the sea with wonderful metallic overtones and lots of umami and salt. After the oyster has gone down your throat there is a lovely meaty aftertaste.

I have been asked hundreds of times what an oyster tastes like. Not an unreasonable question. But like with many things a difficult one to answer, as people's perceptions are different.

Here is a rather overblown description brought down to earth by the editor:

If you don't love life you can't enjoy an oyster; there is a shock of freshness to it and intimations of the ages of man, some piercing intuition of the sea and all its weeds and breezes. They shiver you for a split second. [Just taste like salt to me! – Ed]

Eleanor Clark

The Shellfish Association of Great Britain has created a whole list of taste. Here is what they say about Colchester oysters.

West Mersea

Nose	A clean, fresh faint nose of rockpools (iodine & seaweed)
Body	Well-balanced salt to sweet ratio. Delicate cucumber & lettuce flavour
Finish	Long on the palate, earthy potting soil followed by a lingering tart metallic tang
Texture	Silky, delicate, plump

Flavour 6	**Saltiness 7**	**Sweetness 5**	**Umami 5**

Yes there is the marmite issue. You may hate the taste of oysters. Or like the editor in the quote above only be able to taste salt. Try a couple more and you may find that gradually you start to like and then love them. If not sorry, but oysters are not for you so give the oysters to someone who loves them and sell this book second hand on Amazon.

For a very few people there is the problem of having an allergy to oysters. It's rare but it is worth mentioning. Sadly if you have an allergic reaction you should stop eating oysters. The allergy seems to get worse not better if exposed to more oysters.

This does not include those people who attend the annual Colchester Oyster Feast. They get over excited, stuff themselves silly, drink far more alcohol than they should and blame the subsequent illness on a dodgy oyster. No sir, it was the drink and two helpings of pudding. To be fair one year most of the food they ate was contaminated and to cap it all the oysters were imported from Eire. Perhaps dear reader you can see why I do not approve of this jaded, faded Feast which seems to bring our succulent local oysters into disrepute instead of promoting them.

CHAPTER 4

SEX

Are oysters an aphrodisiac?

Yes is the straight answer. They are good on a dietary level and on a psychological level too.

'Eat oysters love longer' that is what the Americans say. Deserved or not, the oyster has maintained a timeless mystique when it comes to passion. The oysters' own love life is an interesting one, reproducing during the summer months and changing sex every time they do so. A single oyster can incubate up to one million larvae and may do so more than once a year.

In my days selling oysters my bussiness partner and I were always being asked really interesting questions about oysters. Often about their aphrodisiac qualities.

So I have struggled manfully to answer at least some of the questions we were asked. The questions were often asked a bit nudge nudge, wink wink – if they would be good for 'the bedroom' or 'will they perk up my husband'. My business partner, Terry Croucher, had two stock jokes that he would often weave into his reply. 'Well I had a dozen last night but only eleven worked' or 'they certainly put lead in your pencil but you do need somewhere to write.'

On the basis of their zinc content alone oysters are good for sexual health. Increased zinc intake regulates many sexual parts of a man, including prostate, prostatic fluid, and the abundance of sperm. Zinc is found in sperm and men lose between 3mg and 5mg of zinc per ejaculation.

Oysters are the richest source of zinc of any food around. Zinc plays an important role in wound healing and in maintaining a healthy immune system. It also may help to prevent night blindness. Zinc deficiencies are common in alcoholics and people with kidney disease. Oysters are also a good source of other minerals including calcium, magnesium, and iron.

So stock up on the zinc now folks. Eat more oysters!

Tyrosine, an important amino acid, is also found in oysters. These acids heighten the amount of dopamine in the brain. This is what makes a person get things done. It also is vital to stimulate the brain for sexual desire.

A good healthy diet helps a healthy sexual appetite. Oysters are one of the most nutritionally well-balanced foods. They contain protein, carbohydrates and lipids. They are an excellent source of vitamins A, B1 (thiamin), B2 (riboflavin), B3 (niacin), C and D.

Oysters have been linked with love and sexuality for thousands of years.

The word 'aphrodisiac' comes from Aphrodite, the Greek goddess of love, said to have sprung forth from the sea on an oyster shell and the mother of Eros. Because Aphrodite was said to be born from the foam of the sea, many types of seafood have reputations as aphrodisiacs.

Many ancient people believed in the so-called 'law of similarity', reasoning that an object resembling genitalia may possess sexual powers. Ginseng, rhinoceros horn, and oysters are three classical examples.

Back in second century AD, a satire by Juvenal, a Roman satirist, mentioned that the Romans documented oysters as an aphrodisiac food. In fact, Juvenal wrote about the reckless ways of women after they had ingested wine and ate 'giant oysters'.

The dashing lover Casanova also used to start a meal by eating twelve dozen oysters. In his memoirs he admitted seducing 122, giving his own take on a serving suggestion in Volume Six: 'I placed the shell on the edge of her lips and after a good deal of laughing, she sucked in the oyster, which she held between her lips. I instantly recovered it by placing my lips on hers.'

Charming oysters I cry:
My masters, come buy,
So plump and so fresh,
So sweet is their flesh,
No Colchester oyster
Is sweeter and moister:
Your stomach they settle,
And rouse up your mettle:
They'll make you a dad
Of a lass or a lad;
And madam your wife
They'll please to the life;
Be she barren, be she old,
Be she slut, or be she scold,
Eat my oysters, and lie near her,
She'll be fruitful, never fear her.

Jonathan Swift

CHAPTER 5

SELECTION, PREPARATION AND STORAGE

Unlike most shellfish, oysters can have a fairly long shelf life: up to four weeks. However, their taste becomes less pleasant as they age. Oysters should be refrigerated out of water, not frozen, and in 100% humidity. Always store cup side down.

The most important thing to remember when buying fresh, live in the shell oysters to eat at home is that they're still alive. That's vital.

Their shells should be closed and, when tapped, should not make a hollow sound. Smell oysters before buying them. If they smell dank, fishy or rotten, don't buy them.

Eat oysters as soon as possible after buying them, within three to four days. They taste better the fresher they are.

Ideally, oysters should be stored at 40 degrees Fahrenheit until you're ready to eat them. The fridge will do though. Put the oysters on a tray or plate with the round cup side of the oyster down. Cover them with a damp towel or cloth.

Do not soak live oysters in water. (You can rinse them in cold water before shucking.) Oysters stored in water under refrigeration will open, consume available oxygen and die.

Do not store oysters in a plastic bag or sealable container. They will suffocate.

However long you store your oysters make sure that they are still alive. If they are open and do not close when you tap them with a knife they are dead. Throw them away.

Allison Fishman recently wrote about oyster storage online, after Erik Braun contacted her to say that proper storage would keep fresh oysters alive for months at home. Oysters live in the cupped part of the shell, so to store, he suggested keeping them in a cold part of your refrigerator where they can breathe cupped-side down.

She went on to say:

> *Keeping oysters alive for months seemed preposterous to me, so I looked for validation on the web. Most sites recommend storing them for no more than seven days – Linton Seafood was willing to go up to two weeks. Only British sites like Martins Seafresh mentioned the cupped-side trick. Readers of the UK Guardian inquired about the same long-term storage rumour that I heard, and they're still waiting for an answer.*
>
> *As an inquisitive and perhaps foolish woman, I'm putting it to the test: I've now consumed oysters that were one month old and have lived to write about it. The flavour is increasingly intense, like an aged steak. Though an intense oyster is not necessarily a good thing, learning how to keep them lively is.*

The Romans certainly transported them over great distances by boat and cart which would have been weeks at least.

CHAPTER 6

ARE OYSTERS 'GREEN'? ETHICAL CONSIDERATIONS

The oyster is considered by some ethicists to be a really good food choice for those concerned with animal rights, arguing it is acceptable to eat oysters due to their lack of a central nervous system and the generally sustainable and environmentally friendly way in which they are raised and harvested.

One common ethical objection to the consumption of animals is that their cultivation is environmentally harmful. Regarding environmental impact, 95% of oysters are sustainably farmed and harvested (other bivalves are frequently harvested by harmful dredging), feed on plankton (very low on the food chain), and in fact improve the marine environment by removing toxins. As such, farmed oysters are listed as a 'Best Choice' (highest rating) on the Seafood Watch list.

Oysters have been cultured since Roman times and before. Two methods are commonly used, release and bagging. In both cases oysters are cultivated onshore to the size of spat, when they can attach themselves to a substrate. They may be allowed to mature further to form seed oysters. In either case they are then placed in the water to mature.

The release technique involves distributing the spat throughout existing oyster beds allowing them to mature naturally to be collected like wild oysters.

Bagging has the cultivator putting spat in racks or bags and keeping them above the bottom. Harvesting involves simply lifting the bag or rack to the surface and removing the mature oysters. The latter method prevents losses to some predators, but is more expensive.

In the United Kingdom, the native variety (particularly the Colchester native, Ostrea edulis) is still held to be the finest requiring five years to mature and protected by an Act of Parliament during the May–August spawning season. The current market is dominated by the larger Pacific (gigas) oyster and rock oyster varieties, which are farmed year round.

Members of the genus Ostrea are bisexual, that is, they alternate between being male and female during the course of a single breeding season. During a female phase, the oyster deposits eggs within the shell, and sperm is released when the same oyster switches to a male phase and fertilizes these eggs. After a twelve-day period of incubation, the larval oysters, or spat, swim away from the parent in search of their own place to settle.

The Oyster Girl by Karl Gussow, 1882

CHAPTER 7

A BIT OF LITERATURE SEASONED WITH A BIT OF CULTURE

Basket of Oysters

As I was walking down a London Street,
A pretty little oyster girl, I chanced for to meet.
I lifted up her basket and boldly I did peek,
Just to see if she's got any oysters.

Chorus:

'Oysters, Oysters, Oysters', said she.
'These are the finest oysters that you will ever see.
I'll sell them three-a-penny but I give 'em to you free,
'Cause I see you're a lover of oysters.'

'Landlord, Landlord, Landlord', says I.
'Have you got a little room that's empty and nearby.
Where me and the pretty little oyster girl may lie,
when we bargain for her basket of oysters.'

We hadn't been upstairs for a quarter hour more,
when that pretty little oyster girl opened up the door,
She picked my pockets and then down the stair she tore,
She left with her basket of oysters.

'Landlord, Landlord, Landlord', I cried.
'Did you see that little oyster girl drinking by my side?
She's gone and picked my pocket', but the landlord just replied,
'You shouldn't be so fond of your oysters.'

Now all you young men be advised by me,
If you meet a pretty oyster girl and you would merry be,
Sew the pockets of your trousers and throw away the key,
Or you'll never get a taste of her oysters.

In similar rollicking style is 'The Oyster Girl' of which there are printed copies dating back to 1820 and examples as far apart as Aberdeen, Somerset and North Carolina. There are variations sometimes called 'The Basket of Oysters', 'The Basket of Eggs' or 'Eggs in her Basket'. Obviously the oyster girl's reputation as a saucy trickster was well established. Shakespeare was fluent. In The Merry Wives of Windsor, he has Pistol saying:

Why, then the world's mine oyster.
Which I with sword will open

In Richard II:

Off goes his bonnet to an oyster wench

Then this intriguing line in Much Ado:

Love may transform me to an oyster

Then there is this curious and haunting image from As You Like It when Touchstone pronounces:

Rich honesty dwells like a miser, sir, in a poor house; as your pearl in your foul oyster

And King Lear's Fool jests:

Canst tell how an oyster makes his shell?

Today's theatre audiences tend to sustain themselves by craftily tucking into goodies during the performance or quaffing pre-ordered drinks at the bar during the interval.

Shakespeare's audience ate oysters, thousands of them during, in between and after the performance. The preferred snacks for Tudor theatre-goers appear to have been, according to archeologists, oysters, crabs, cockles, mussels, periwinkles and whelks, as well as walnuts, hazelnuts, raisins, plums, cherries, dried figs and peaches.

In today's Globe Theatre eating is discouraged with stern looks from staff in modern aprons. No oysters or any of the Tudor favourites. A real shame that they don't enter into the real spirit of Shakespeare's time as food was so important to the whole experience for the Tudors.

Dickens was also fluent in the subject of oysters

'Can you open me an oyster, my dear?' said Mr. John Dounce. 'Dare say I can, sir,' replied the lady in blue, with playfulness. And Mr. John Dounce eat one oyster, and then looked at the young lady, and then eat another, and then squeezed the young lady's hand as she was opening the third, and so forth, until he had devoured a dozen of those at eight pence in less than no time.

'Can you open me half-a-dozen more, my dear?' inquired Mr. John Dounce.

'I'll see what I can do for you, sir,' replied the young lady in blue, even more bewitchingly than before; and Mr. John Dounce eat half-a-dozen more of those at eight pence.

Charles Dickens 'The Misplaced Attachment of Mr. John Dounce' in Sketches from Boz.

Secret, self-contained, and as solitary as an oyster.

Charles Dickens, A Christmas Carol

There's nothing in Christianity or Buddhism that quite matches the sympathetic unselfishness of an oyster.

Saki

From the Romans onwards oysters appear in literature.

Oysters are not really food, but are relished to bully the sated stomach into further eating.

Seneca

Oysters we ate,
sweet blue babies,
twelve eyes looked up at me,
running with lemon and Tabasco.
I was afraid to eat this father-food
and Father laughed and drank down his martini,
clear as tears.
It was a soft medicine
that came from the sea into my mouth,
moist and plump.

I swallowed.
It went down like a large pudding.
Then I ate one o'clock and two o'clock.
Then I laughed and then we laughed
and let me take note –
there was a death,
the death of childhood
there at the Union Oyster House
for I was fifteen
and eating oysters
and the child was defeated.
The woman won.

Anne Sexton, from 'Death of the Fathers, 1. Oysters'

He had often eaten oysters, but had never had enough.

W. S. Gilbert

You needn't tell me that a man who doesn't love oysters and
asparagus and good wines has got a soul, or a stomach either. He's
simply got the instinct for being unhappy.

Saki

At the end of a sentence I call for tea
At the end of a paragraph, bread and b.
At the end of a page, chip potatoes and hake
At the end of a chapter, fillet steak
But ah! when I finish the ultimate line
When I've brought to fulfillment the grand design
When I look at the thing and it's mine, all mine
Then it's Oysters, my love, with Cold White Wine!

Jan Morris, Writers' Favourite Recipes (1978)

An oyster lives a dreadful but exciting life. Indeed, his chance to live at all is slim, and if he should survive the arrows of his own outrageous fortune and in the two weeks of his youth find a clean smooth place to fix on, the years afterwards are full of stress, passion and danger.

M. F. K. Fisher, Consider the Oyster (1941)

'A loaf of bread,' the Walrus said,
'Is what we chiefly need:
Pepper and vinegar besides
Are very good indeed –
Now, if you're ready, Oysters dear,
We can begin to feed.'
But answer there came none –

And this was scarcely odd because
They'd eaten every one.

Lewis Carroll, Through the Looking Glass

As I ate the oysters with their strong taste of the sea and their faint metallic taste that the cold white wine washed away, leaving only the sea taste and the succulent texture, and as I drank their cold liquid from each shell and washed it down with the crisp taste of the wine, I lost the empty feeling [from finishing a story] and began to be happy and to make plans.

Ernest Hemingway, A Moveable Feast

The deep sea suckled me, the waves sounded over me; rollers were my coverlet as I rested on my bed. I have no feet and frequently open my mouth to the flood. Sooner or later some man will consume me, who cares nothing for my shell. With the point of his knife he will pierce me through, ripping the skin away from my side, and straight away eat me uncooked as I am...

Riddle number 77, in the Old English Exeter Book, first made public in 1072 by Leofric, first Bishop of Exeter. The answer is 'an Oyster'.

There once was an oyster
whose story I tell,
who found that some sand
had gotten into his shell.
It was only a grain,
but it gave him great pain,
for oysters have feelings
although they're so plain.

Now, did he berate
the harsh workings of fate
that had brought him
to such a deplorable state?
Did he curse at the government,
Cry for election,
and claim that the sea should
have given him protection?

'No,' he said to himself
as he lay on a shell,
since I cannot remove it,
I shall try to improve it.
Now the years have rolled around,
as the years always do,
and he came to his ultimate destiny ... Stew!

And the small grain of sand
that had bothered him so
was a beautiful pearl
all richly aglow.

Now the tale has a moral:
For isn't it grand
what an oyster can do
with a morsel of sand?

What couldn't we do
if we'd only begin
with some of the things
that get under our skin.

Anon

'*Not a very nice neighbourhood this, sir' said Sam, with a touch of*
the hat, which always preceded his entering into conversation with
his master.
'*It is not indeed, Sam,' replied Mr Pickwick, surveying the crowded*
and filthy street through which they were passing.
'*It's a very remarkable circumstance, sir,' said Sam, 'that poverty*
and oysters always seems to go together.'
'*I don't understand, Sam,' said Mr Pickwick.*
'*What I mean, sir,' said Sam, 'is, that the poorer a place is, the*
greater call there seems to be for oysters. Look here, sir; here's a
oyster stall to every half dozen houses. The streets lined vith 'em.
Blessed if I don't think that ven a man's wery poor, he rushes out of
his lodgings and eats oysters in reg'lar desperation.'

Charles Dickens, The Pickwick Papers

CHAPTER 8
DRINKS WITH OYSTERS

People seem to have some pretty fixed views on what to drink with fresh uncooked oysters.

When you see this delicate, silky, briny, complex flavoured mollusc in its half shell it does cry out for good champagne. But good stout is also excellent, as is Fino, and some lagers really work well. It is very much your own taste which is important. The following are simply suggestions for you to explore as to the delightful flavours which can be conjured from the oyster by the drink that accompanies this amazing mollusc.

The oyster has its own terroir. As the tasting notes show it can vary from buttery to salty, from sweet to umami. So different oysters can be paired with different drinks. Experimentation can be fun!

What about cooked oysters? Well they are much more forgiving. Many more drinks can be paired with them, dependant on the rest of the ingredients used.

There's more than one outstanding match plus some good alternatives you may not have thought of. Which one you choose will obviously depend on your own taste, which after all is the only important factor.

Fino sherry, bone dry, chilled of course, is a brilliant drink for virtually all oyster and shellfish dishes. Fino goes well with Angels on Horseback, all of the fried oyster dishes and I just love Fino with lots of the cooked dishes.

Chablis nicely chilled is one of the top choices. There are actually fossilized oyster shells in the soil of the Chablis region. This should give you a hint that Chablis should hit the spot. And it does for fresh oysters. Incidentally if you are lucky enough to be eating Colchester natives push the boat out and buy a premier cru.

Brut (dry) Champagne is a grand choice. Do not be tempted by anything but the brutist of the bruts – sweet does not work. Ultra dry champagnes like Laurent Perrier Ultra Brut and Drappier Brut Nature that don't have any dosage (sugar and wine solution) added to them before bottling work best though lighter styles of regular non-vintage Champagne such as Taittinger will do a perfectly good job. The bubbles create the magic, the perfect textural contrast to the smooth velvety texture of the oysters even when cooked.

Prosecco and Cava sparkling wine, again ultra dry, are also the best match by far for deep-fried oysters. Many people now argue that Prosecco is often better and cheaper than some champagne. The same goes for Cava, which is now a firm favourite with the Brits.

English wine its time to try these new and excellent sparkling wines, which have taken the wine world by storm. Some English sparkling wines now give champagne a run for its money. But they are still too expensive and the government needs to look at tax structures to make them competitive.

Muscadet, bone dry, flinty slightly metallic clean-as-a-whistle – a perfect wine for all shellfish. The best wines come from the Sèvre-et-Maine region and are labelled 'sur lie' (the wine is aged on the lees, the residue of the yeast used to ferment the wine which gives it more flavour).

Also in this category of bone-dry whites comes **Picpoul de Pinet** from the south of France, Pinot Grigio from Italy and Albariño from Galicia in Northern Spain.

Sauvignon Blanc is what they would drink round Bordeaux, also an oyster-producing area. Stick to young and unoaked versions. The added zestiness of Sauvignon also helps with strong seasonings like shallot and red wine vinegar or Tabasco.

Chardonnay is good with the more buttery flavoured oysters and with creamy sauces. Choose a lightly oaked, creamy style such as you find in Burgundy, Limoux in southern France or cool climate regions of the New World.

Oyster stout should be tried in its own right but it is of course a natural choice for drinking with oysters.

Oysters have had a long association with stout. When stouts were emerging in the 18th century, oysters were a commonplace food often served in public houses and taverns.

Modern oyster stouts may be made with a handful of oysters in the barrel, hence the claim of one establishment, the Porterhouse Brewery in Dublin, that their award-winning Oyster Stout was not suitable for vegetarians.

Others, such as Marston's Oyster Stout, use the name with the implication that the beer would be suitable for drinking with oysters. The Mersea Island Brewery situated on the same coastline as the Colchester oyster beds hits the right notes with its oyster stout which is excellent with oysters.

Guinness is another wonderful stout, classic and available almost everywhere. The saltiness of the oysters counteracts the bitterness of the beer. I tried a 'black velvet' – champagne and Guinness – in Brighton. Not sure whether it ruined good champagne or ruined the Guinness but it was an expensive mistake.

There are some lagers made with champagne yeast which go well with oysters cooked and raw. Chapel Down vineyard's Curious Brew from

Kent for instance is excellent.

If you are not drinking alcohol any good sparkling water with a slice of lemon is good. Also I love to drink **tomato juice**, especially Big Tom spiced.

Tomato juice brings me onto a mixture of both drink and oysters. The Oyster Shot. My chum and business partner, Terry Croucher, makes the best Bloody Mary in the world. He also makes one called a Bleeding Mary with added chilli. No point in asking – he refuses to divulge the recipe. The recipe for an Oyster Shot is below.

OYSTER SHOT

Ingredients

> 250 ml vodka (Stolichnaya for choice)
> 375 ml Big Tom or any other good tomato juice
> 1 dash of Worcestershire sauce, to taste
> 1 dash of Tabasco, to taste (or other hot chilli sauce of your choice)
> 1 pinch celery salt, to taste
> 1 dash of lemon juice, to taste
> 10 oysters
> 1 stalk of celery, finely shredded

Method

1. Mix the vodka and tomato juice and then add the Worcestershire sauce, Tabasco, celery salt and lemon juice to taste.

2. Put an oyster in the bottom of each of ten shot glass, pour over the Bloody Mary, and garnish with a few celery strands before serving.

CHAPTER 9
OYSTER RECIPES

This first recipe is a bit of fun for me and I hope for you. Try it though – it is really good! Remember that basic instructions on opening oysters are included in Chapter 2.

OYSTRES EN GRAUEY

I suspect this means oysters in gravy. This is the oldest English recipe (or receipt) I have included. It is quite complicated but surprisingly delicious. Almonds were used as a thickener for centuries. You could use bought almond milk and ignore the white wine to make it easier. I have put in the original recipe for fun.

ORIGINAL RECEIPT circa AD 1500

Take gode Mylke of Almaundys, an drawe it wyth Wyne an gode Fysshe brothe, an sette it on the fyre, & lat boyle; & caste ther-to Clowes, Maces, Sugre an powder Gyngere, an a fewe parboylid Oynonys y-mynsyd; than take fayre Oystrys, & parboyle hem in fayre Water, & caste hem ther-to, an lete hem boyle to-gederys; & thanne serue hem forth. (Don't worry the translation is below.)

Ingredients

24 oysters
3 cups almond milk, made with dry wine *
1 cup fish stock
1 medium onion, minced
2 teaspoons sugar
¼ teaspoon powdered ginger
⅛ teaspoon cloves
⅛ teaspoon mace

Method

1. Open the oysters, keep as much of the liquor as possible and add at stage 4.

2. In a saucepan, over high heat, bring water to a boil, and parboil the shucked oysters for about 5 minutes, or until they are nearly done. Drain.

3. In a large pot, over medium heat, combine almond milk, minced onions, fish stock, spices and sugar. Bring to a boil, reduce heat, and simmer, stirring constantly, for about 20 minutes, or until the onions are done.

4. Stir in the parboiled oysters. Simmer, stirring frequently, for another 10 minutes. If the almond milk starts to get too thick, add more stock or wine. Serve in individual bowls.

*Almond Milk

Ingredients

1 cup raw almonds
3 cups dry white wine

Method

1. Soak the almonds in water overnight.

2. Drain the water from the almonds and discard.

3. Using a blender blend the 3 cups of wine with the almonds until almost smooth.

4. Strain the blended almond mixture using cheesecloth or other strainer.

Homemade raw almond milk will keep well in the refrigerator for three or four days.

BAIAN STEW

Now let's go back in time to the Romans.

I have adapted this ancient Roman recipe so that a modern cook can get all the ingredients.

Some of the salt and sweet flavours may seem a little confused to our palate but once together they work well.

It should really have jellyfish in it but you have to soak them in vinegar to neutralize the venom so I have omitted them.

Also I have substituted sweet sherry (or you could even use port) for the Roman 'passum' which was raisin wine. Most importantly I have substituted nam pla (Asian fish sauce) for the Roman 'garum'.

Garum is ubiquitous in Roman cooking but no longer made today. Think of soy sauce from Oriental cooking and you will get an idea how widespread its use was. It was made from fish guts, blood or indeed whole fish left to ferment in sealed containers. I have added a half teaspoon of oregano into the recipe as the garum frequently had this but we cannot hope to replicate the subtlety of the Roman sauce with its many variations and herbs.

The Roman historian and writer Tacitus tells us that this stew was served at a banquet given by Nero in the fashionable town of Baiae. His mother Agrippina was a guest. Nero had ordered the boat which was to transport her home to be sabotaged. Indeed it did sink but she managed to swim to safety and survived. You can ponder on mans inhumanity to even his own mum as you enjoy this stew.

Right sleeves rolled up now have a go!

Ingredients

20 oysters
20 clams
40 mussels
For the sauce
40g roasted pine nuts
2 celery stalks
1 handful of lovage leaf
1 cup dry white wine
10 pitted dates, chopped
1 tablespoon nam pla mixed with ½ teaspoon dried oregano
½ teaspoon pepper
½ teaspoon coriander
½ teaspoon cumin
1 tablespoon of sweet sherry
1 tablespoon olive oil

Method

1. Open the oysters.

2. Put the liquid from the oysters and the white wine in a pan and gently heat the mussels and clams in batches in the combined liquids. As soon as the molluscs open take them out and remove the meat from the shells. Put the meats back in the warm liquid.

3. Chop the pine nuts and celery finely. Cook for 10 minutes in the olive oil in a separate pan.

4. Add the pine nut and celery mixture, and the oysters, to the pan with the liquids.

5. Cook gently, stirring from time to time, for about 30 minutes.

STEAK, KIDNEY, OYSTER AND STOUT PUDDING

Now for the BIG ONE – that great British pudding. Warming and wonderful and with flavour that will knock your hat off!

You will need a 1.8 litre pudding basin.

Ingredients

For the suet dough
300g self-raising flour
2 pinches sea salt
150g suet
about 200ml cold water
For the filling
150ml good stout. Drink the rest of the bottle!
150ml beef stock made with a good stock cube
700g rump steak, cut into 3cm cubes
300g ox liver cut into 3cm cubes and soaked in about a litre of milk and a teaspoon of salt for about three hours to take away any bitterness. Wash in water and dry thoroughly.
4 pinches Maldon sea salt
4 pinches freshly ground black pepper
2 tablespoons plain flour
1 medium onion, sliced
180g field mushrooms, sliced
14 large gigas oysters, shucked. Try and keep as much liquid as you can and bung it in with the other ingredients.

Method

1. For the suet dough, place the flour, salt and suet in a large bowl, mix them together, and then stir in enough water to make firm dough. Add more water or flour as needed to achieve the right consistency.

2. Turn the dough onto a floured board and roll out a large circle about 0.5cm thick. Cut a quarter segment out of the circle and set it to one side. Use the rolled out dough to line a buttered 1.8 litre pudding basin, allowing a generous overhang at the rim. Press firmly along the seam to ensure a good seal.

3. For the filling, put the stout in a small pan and bring to the boil. Add the beef stock to the stout.

4. Place the steak and kidney in a large bowl and season with the salt and freshly ground black pepper. Add the flour and toss to coat the meat.

5. Add the onions and mushrooms to the bowl and mix well with the meat.

6. Layer the meat mixture with the oysters into the pudding basin, ensuring the filling is tightly packed.

7. Mix the oyster juices with the wine and stout and pour into the pudding basin until it almost covers the filling.

8. Roll out the reserved dough to make a lid, place it on top of the pudding and fold the overhanging dough over, using a little water to act as glue. Press along the join to make a tight seal.

9. Cover the pudding loosely with tin foil, leaving room for the pudding to rise slightly, and tie the foil to the basin with string, making a looped handle as you do so.

10. Place the pudding in a steamer or on an upturned saucer in a large saucepan of simmering water loosely covered with a lid, and steam for at least five hours. Add more boiling water to the pan during cooking as needed to prevent the pan from boiling dry.

CRISPY BESPOKE OYSTERS

This is one of the simplest and best recipes ever. I was introduced to this quick and easy recipe by my brilliant chef chums at Bespoke Caterers. Panko makes such an easy crisp coating. You can even buy panko on Amazon these days. It's also in Waitrose.

Ingredients

12 fresh oysters
4–6 tablespoons flour
1–2 eggs, beaten
1 cup of panko breadcrumbs seasoned with salt and freshly ground pepper
2–3 tablespoons vegetable oil

Method

1. Shuck the oysters and place in a colander to drain.

2. Pat the oysters dry with kitchen paper and dust with the flour.

3. Dip the floured oysters in beaten eggs, then in the seasoned panko breadcrumbs (coat each oyster thoroughly).

4. Heat the vegetable oil in a thick bottomed frying pan until quite hot.

5. Fry the oysters until golden brown on one side, 1–2 minutes, then carefully turn over.

6. Fry on the other side until golden brown, another 2 minutes. Don't overcook.

Remove from the pan and return the cooked oysters to their half shells or pop them on a little dressed salad.

7. Serve immediately.

OYSTERS OLIVER

I worked with Jamie Oliver on the Colchester Pudding. An amazing claim to fame I hear you cry. The few minutes on the box with the young Jamie and our chum Jimmy Doherty created more emails, Facebook and Twitter comments than I have had in the whole of my life. Bloody marvellous, you produce a massively successful food and drink festival – nothing. A few minutes on TV with a celeb – instant praise!

He pimped my pudding so I am pimping his recipe. Seriously, I really admire Jamie Oliver. He is a great man and a great chef.

You will see in some of this and other recipes a call for horseradish or horseradish sauce. By this I mean freshly fine grated horseradish root lightly dressed with wine vinegar. Some of you will however prefer the full sauce and you can find lots of recipes with varying complexity online.

Fresh horseradish goes wonderfully with oysters and of course beef and lots of other food. It is a beautiful mix with mustard. A ready-made version is Tewkesbury mustard.

Horseradish is however not always easy to buy. In a small Czech town I happened upon a Tesco Express. In the spirit of enquiry I went in and there were pounds of horseradish on sale. On my return I went into my local Tesco Superstore and they told me they hadn't stocked fresh horseradish for years. You can buy it online from Ocado and Amazon.

Just looking at the ingredients in the bottled ready-made versions should put you off ever sullying your palate, so buy fresh or not at all is my advice.

OK now for the recipe!

Ingredients

24 gigas (Pacific oysters) NOT NATIVES JAMIE!!
100g flour
170ml really cold water
1 fresh egg white whisked until it is stiff
1 tablespoon olive oil. I prefer good Spanish olive oil.
1 litre vegetable oil
For the dressing
12 ripe tomatoes peeled (put in heat proof bowl, cut skin with a cross, pour over boiling water. Leave for 10 minutes then peel off skin).
2 tablespoons of horseradish sauce.
1 clove of garlic, peeled
1 or 2 tablespoons of white wine vinegar to taste. Good stuff please it has a milder acid flavour than cheap ones. I would use just one tablespoon as I prefer a milder vinegar hit.
2, 3, or even 4 drops of Tabasco to taste
Maldon sea salt and freshly ground pepper
To serve - Rocket leaves

Method

1. Open the oysters. Put the oyster meat in a bowl and scrub and reserve the cup half of each shell.

2. Whisk the flour with the very cold water. Then carefully fold in the stiff egg whites before gently adding in a tablespoon of olive oil.

3. Next put the tomatoes, horseradish, garlic, and one tablespoon of vinegar into a blender and blend till nice and smooth.

4. Taste the mix. Now add a drop of Tabasco. Taste. Add more Tabasco if needed. Taste. Now add more wine vinegar if you think it is needed. Give it all a good stir. Now blend the mixture again till very smooth.

5. Put a little pile of salt for each half shell on a serving plate. Balance a half shell on each pile so it remains level. Divide the dressing equally into each of the half shells.

6. Heat the oil in a deep fat fryer to 180ºC. Fry the rocket in small batches for about 25 seconds until it is crisp. Let it drain on kitchen paper.

7. Now put each oyster in the batter. With a spoon carefully drop each one in the hot oil. Do not crowd the pan. After 2 minutes they should be nicely golden brown. Remove each one from the hot oil with a slotted spoon and drain briefly on kitchen paper.

8. Now equally divide the fried rocket in place on the top of the dressing in each half shell. Place a fried oyster on each and serve immediately.

PO-BOYS

An absolute classic oyster dish from the US of A. It is very popular and one of the best recipes going to get people into cooked oysters. I have included two recipes of this important dish.

Fried Oyster Po-Boys 1

The real benefit of this recipe is that the cornmeal crust not only gives a good texture and flavour but it 'seals' the oyster so that it cooks lightly in its own juices, and little of the oil is absorbed by the crust.

Ingredients

2 dozen shucked large oysters
1 tablespoon salt
1 teaspoon black pepper
½ teaspoon cayenne
1 teaspoon of very finely chopped (to the point of mashed) garlic
4 eggs, beaten
2 cups of cornmeal
sunflower oil
2–3 French sticks, cut in half
butter for bread
chilli sauce of your choice

Method

1. Cut the top off the loaves lengthwise.

2. Drain the oysters and dry them on kitchen paper.

3. Sprinkle seasoning over oysters and mix them well.

4. Dip the oysters into the beaten eggs, then the cornmeal.

5. Lightly sprinkle with salt and pepper and set aside in the refrigerator for two hours.

6. Remove from the refrigerator and dip in egg and cornmeal again.

7. Fry in hot oil (180°C–200°C) until golden brown. Remove from oil and drain oysters on kitchen paper.

8. Brush loaves (top and bottom) with melted butter and place in a hot oven. Heat until edges start to get crisp.

9. Remove from oven and fill loaves with fried oysters. Add sauce piquante to taste. Replace loaf top and enjoy.

OYSTERS PO' BOYS 2 (À LA HAIRY BIKERS)

This is more complicated than 1 but wonderfully satisfying. The remoulade is really great. I suggest you check your cupboard for ingredients for this one before you start, but all of the ingredients are easily available.

When I first met the Hairy Bikers I was wearing a Che Guevara T-shirt. They gave it an odd look. I asked them why. They both rolled up their sleeves and they have identical tattoos of Che's iconic image on their upper arms!

Ingredients

18 freshly shucked oysters
sunflower oil, for deep frying
For the remoulade
1 small jar mayonnaise, or make your own
1 tablespoon chopped fresh tarragon
1 tablespoon capers
1 tablespoon finely chopped shallots
1 teaspoon Dijon mustard
dash Tabasco
1 tablespoon tomato purée
2 tablespoons lemon juice
1 teaspoon red wine vinegar
½ teaspoon cayenne pepper
1 tablespoon horseradish sauce (there are lots of good recipes online for horseradish sauce, they all refer to grated horseradish and should all say finely grated and the finer the better)
For the cornmeal crust
225g cornmeal
1 tablespoon ground cumin
1 teaspoon ground fennel
1 teaspoon cayenne pepper

salt and freshly ground black pepper
For the egg wash
2 eggs
285ml milk
To serve
French stick, warmed
butter
crisp lettuce, such as little gem or cos

Method

1. To make the remoulade mix all the ingredients together. Taste and adjust any of the ingredients you think necessary.

2. For the cornmeal crust, combine all the ingredients in a bowl. Add salt and freshly ground black pepper to taste.

3. In a separate bowl, combine the egg and milk for the egg wash.

4. Dry the freshly shucked oysters with kitchen towel then dip in the egg wash and then in the cornmeal crust mixture, coating liberally.

5. Heat the vegetable oil in a large pan for deep frying until a breadcrumb sizzles gently in it.

6. Deep-fry the coated oysters until golden, about 2–3 minutes. Remove with a slotted spoon and drain on kitchen towel.

7. Take a freshly warmed French stick, split down the middle and butter. Top with a layer of lettuce then drizzle over the remoulade sauce. Add the deep-fried oysters and cover with the other half of the French loaf.

8. Whack into this wonderful warm long sandwich as quickly as you can.

ANGELS ON HORSEBACK

These are great as a little party snack, or served as part of a full meal as a savoury.

Nobody really knows where this tasty treat got its name. It has been suggested that it derives from the French 'anges à cheval', and there appears to be no significance in the oyster/angel and bacon/horse links. Its first occurrence in English, according to the Oxford English Dictionary and other sources, is in 1888, in Mrs Beeton's Book of Household Management.

Ingredients

16–32 small oysters or larger ones cut in half, shucked
8–16 slices of thin-cut bacon
16–32 wooden toothpicks
3–4 limes or lemons

Method

1. Working in batches if necessary, cook the bacon slices on medium low heat in a large frying pan, until only about halfway cooked, but not crispy. You need to pre-cook the bacon a bit or else when you cook it with the oysters the oysters will be overcooked by the time the bacon is crispy. Set the bacon aside to cool.

2. Preheat the grill to hot.

3. To make an angel on horseback, wrap ½ a piece of bacon around the small oyster and secure it with a toothpick. Overlap the edges of the bacon by about 2.5cm if you can.

4. Place under a hot grill to cook the oyster and crisp the bacon, about 5–6 minutes on the first side, another 2–4 once you turn them over. You will need to turn them once or twice to get a good crispiness on all sides.

5. As soon as they come off the heat, squirt with the lemon or lime juice and serve hot.

BAKED OYSTERS WITH MOZZARELLA

Please try and buy British asparagus, the flavour is far superior. Also go for real mozzarella as the texture is so much better.

Ingredients

6 fresh oysters, cleaned and shucked
2 streaky bacon rashers, finely chopped
30g celery, finely chopped
4 asparagus tips, finely chopped
salt and black pepper
30g finely chopped mozzarella cheese

Method

1. In a small pan cook the bacon for 1–2 minutes until crispy. Add the celery and asparagus.

2. Season.

3. Spoon the bacon and asparagus mixture over the oysters. Sprinkle over the cheese.

4. Cook the oysters under a medium grill for 3–4 minutes until the cheese melts and is golden brown.

Oysters with Passion Fruit and Lavender Jelly

Heston Blumenthal pioneered this recipe. Horseradish goes really well with oysters as I have mentioned earlier. More surprising is that so does lavender. Although actually quite easy to make, this isn't one for the faint-hearted cook. Take care to follow the instructions.

Ingredients

12 oysters (use gigas for this recipe and they need to be a good size)
For the horseradish cream
2 tablespoons mayonnaise
25ml whipped cream
25ml horseradish sauce
For the jelly
1 gelatin leaf
120ml oyster juice (this is from the oysters when you open them)
30ml water
60ml passion fruit juice (available from all good supermarkets)
brown sugar (to taste)
48 pieces dried food-grade lavender (available at good health-food shops)

Method

1. Carefully shuck the oysters and remove from their shells (keep the juice). Cut in half. Drain on kitchen paper and reserve. Thoroughly clean the shells.

2. For the horseradish cream, place all the ingredients in a bowl and mix together.

3. To make the jelly, soften the gelatin by soaking it for a couple of minutes in cold water. Mix the oyster juice, water and passion fruit juice, then add sugar to taste. Warm a little of this in a pan, add the softened gelatin and stir until it is dissolved. Pour in the rest of the liquid and stir well. Pass through a fine sieve, then reserve.

4. To assemble the dish, place a small amount of the horseradish cream in the base of each oyster shell, place one oyster on the top and press lightly to secure. Leave to set in the fridge for about 15 minutes, and then gently pour over the jelly until the oysters are just covered. Leave to set in the fridge.

5. To serve, place two pieces of dried lavender on each jelly.

BAKED OYSTER AND FILLET STEAK

This is really good, huge on taste and with a brilliant texture. This is a real celebration dish, which will repay close attention to detail and hard work. Some people suggest that this either ruins a good steak or in the alternative ruins some good oysters. I don't agree I think oysters and beef go remarkably well together.

Ingredients

500g beef fillet, trimmed
150ml stout
150ml strong beef or veal stock
2 shallots, chopped
1 bay leaf
1 teaspoon brown sugar
25g butter
salt and pepper
16 oysters, shucked

Method

1. Poach the whole piece of fillet in a mixture of the stout and stock with the chopped shallots and bay leaf for about 10 minutes (the beef should be rare in the middle).

2. Remove the meat and keep warm.

3. Add the sugar to the stock mixture and reduce by about one third, finally adding the butter to make the sauce thick and shiny.

4. Season to taste with salt and pepper.

5. Pop the oysters into the sauce for one minute and then remove.

6. Pour the sauce on to white plates, then slice the beef thinly and arrange decoratively. Garnish each portion with the poached oysters.

FLOUNDER AND OYSTERS RECIPE

A little fishy dishy. Simple and lovely. Avoid overcooking.

Ingredients

8 fillets of flounder
16 oysters, shucked
1 tablespoon parsley, chopped
½ medium onion, chopped
2 tablespoons butter
seasonings to taste

Method

1. Butter a small baking pan or dish.

2. Place chopped onions, fillets of flounder, oysters, butter, chopped parsley and seasonings in baking pan.

3. Bake in a hot oven for about 8–10 minutes.

CREAM OF OYSTER STEW

This tasty stew has a surprise ingredient, Campbell's condensed mushroom soup. This has been a 'cheffie' secret ingredient for years. Do not dilute just bung it in! I used to make 'Chicken in cream sauce and white wine' using Campbell's condensed mushroom soup. Just put chicken pieces in a roasting tin, whack in the soup, add a dollop of cream and a glass or two of white wine, pepper, give it all a stir, cover with foil. Cook in a medium oven for an hour. Lots of praise from customers! There you go – two recipes for the price of one.

Ingredients

4 tablespoons butter
½ cup chopped celery
½ cup chopped onion
½ cup diced carrots
¼ teaspoon white pepper
oyster liquor
1 large can Campbell's cream of mushroom soup
½ cup milk
¼ cup chopped parsley
24 shucked oysters
small glass very dry fino sherry (I like a glass of very cold fino with oysters)

Method

1. Melt the butter in a large sauce pan. Now sauté the celery, onion and carrots in melted butter for 5 minutes.

2. Add the white pepper and the liquor that has been drained from the oysters.

3. Add the mushroom soup and milk; stir until smooth. Heat to a low simmer. Add the parsley and oysters. Heat until the oysters are plump and their edges begin to ruffle.

4. Add a splash of sherry and serve immediately.

STEAMED OYSTER WITH GINGER

Let's get a bit Asian.

Ingredients

1 dozen oysters (on the half shell)
½ cup finely chopped spring onions
½ cup finely chopped fresh ginger
2 cloves garlic, finely chopped
½ cup of butter
salt and pepper to taste

Method

1. Melt the butter, then add ginger, garlic, onions, salt, and pepper. Cook gently in the butter. Do not allow to burn and just soften.

2. Steam the oysters in a steamer for 10 minutes.

3. When the oysters have been steamed, add 1 tablespoon of mixture to each individual oyster and serve hot.

Oyster omelette is a Chinese dish that is widely known in Taiwan, Singapore, and many parts of Asia for its savoury taste. There are lots of variations to this recipe and the first one below comes from Singapore. Oyster Omelette is often sold in night markets, and has constantly been ranked by many foreigners as the top cuisine from Taiwan is the number two recipe below.

Singapore Omelette 1

Ingredients for Oyster Omelette:

12 large shucked oysters
2 tablespoons cornflour
1 tablespoons rice flour
8 tablespoons water
1 tablespoons oil
2 cloves garlic, finely chopped
3 eggs, beaten
1 tablespoons soy sauce
1 tablespoons Japanese sake or Chinese rice wine
1 pinch white pepper
6 sprigs coriander, to garnish
1 spring onion, for garnish

Method:

1. Shuck the oysters. Pat dry with kitchen towel.

2. Mix both cornflour and rice flour together with the water to make a fairly thin batter.

3. Heat a large heavy frying pan until very hot and add oil. Pour in the batter and cook for about 15 seconds until batter is half set before adding in the eggs.

4. When the eggs are almost set, make a hole in the centre by pushing the egg and batter mixture to the side of the pan. Pour in a little more oil and fry the garlic for a few seconds.

5. Mix, and then season with soy sauce, sake and pepper. Add oysters and cook just long enough to heat through.

6. Garnish and serve immediately with fresh coriander leaves and spring onions.

7. And now for the sauce to add to your omelette; make this as hot as you like, increasing the heat by adding more chilli.

Chilli Sauce:

3 whole Large Red Chillies
1 slice 2 mm thick young Ginger
1 clove garlic
2 tbsp vinegar
1 tbsp hot water
1/2 tsp sugar
Salt to taste

Method

Throw all ingredients into a mortar and pestle or a blender, blend until you get a sauce like consistency and taste. Serve with oyster omelette.

TAIWANESE OYSTER OMELETTE 2

Make sauce first and set aside.

Taiwanese Oyster Omelette Sauce

> 3 tablespoons ketchup
> 3 tablespoons soy paste (please note this is the paste not the sauce)
> 2 tablespoons sugar

Method

Place all ingredients in a small bowl, and stir until well combined. Set aside until the omelette is done-- it will thicken as it sits.

Taiwanese Omelette

> ¼ cup tapioca starch. (For many British people tapioca is associated with school dinners as a pudding. It is also one of the ingredients of the famous Colchester pudding, which is wonderful. You can buy tapioca in Waitrose and online.)
> ½ cup cold water
> 1cup Chinese greens—(pak choy) Romaine leaves make a good substitute
> 3 eggs
> 1 pinch ground white pepper
> 1 pinch salt
> 6-shucked oysters patted dry on kitchen towel.
> 3 tablespoons corn oil

Method

1. Stir tapioca starch and water together in a small bowl until you have smooth mix. Set aside.

2. Chop pak choy or Romaine leaves into 1/2-inch pieces and set aside.

3. In another bowl, beat eggs. The tried and true Taiwanese method is using chopsticks, and you don't have to fully combine the yolks and whites.

4. Add salt and white pepper.

5. Set aside.

6. Heat oil in a large non-stick frying pan over medium-high heat.

7. When oil is shimmery, add the tapioca mix and reduce heat to medium.

8. Cook for a minute or two until the colour changes from white to translucent.

9. At this point, reduce heat to low and add beaten eggs. Stir for 10 seconds with chopsticks until coarsely combined.

10. Quickly add oysters and greens on top of eggs and press gently to set.

11. Allow to cook, undisturbed, until slightly golden around the edges.

12. Using two spatulas, carefully flip omelette over in pan. Bring heat back up to medium and allow to cook until oysters are fully cooked and omelette is set, about 5 minutes.

Serve omelette on a plate and drizzle desired amount of sauce on top.

Oysters with a Moroccan Sauce of Roasted Pepper, Lemon, Olives and Fresh Coriander

Ingredients

24 oysters, shucked, liquid reserved
1 Moroccan or other preserved lemon, chopped coarsely
2 red peppers, roasted and cut into 5mm dice
16–20 Moroccan green or black olives, pitted and coarsely chopped (about 1/2 cup)
2 tablespoons coriander, chopped
2 tablespoons fresh lemon juice
½ cup extra-virgin olive oil
sea salt and freshly ground pepper
1 loaf of round, rough bread

Method

1. Combine the first seven ingredients in a bowl. Let the mixture sit in the refrigerator for 2 hours.

2. Bring a frying pan to high heat, with a little sea salt and pepper dancing in the bottom. Add the entire bowl to the frying pan and sauté for about 3 minutes, just until the oysters curl up.

3. Adjust to your taste with more olive oil and a bit of tomato purée to tame it down, or add more olives and lemon juice to jazz it up.

4. Serve one of two ways:

(i) Slice off the top of the bread and hollow it out to form a bowl. Set bread pieces aside. Place bread bowl on large platter and surround with bite-sized bread pieces. Pour contents of the frying pan into the bread bowl and serve.

(ii) Serve oysters and sauce in individual ramekins sided with bread and cheese for a light meal.

PICKLED OYSTERS

Ingredients

5 whole cloves
10 peppercorns
24 fresh shucked oysters, drained and juice reserved
½ cup good cider vinegar
½ cup oyster liquid

Method

1. Add the whole cloves and peppercorns to the vinegar and the oyster liquid.

2. Bring the mixture to boiling. Add the oysters and simmer until the oysters curl.

3. Cool and then chill in the refrigerator until ready to serve.

Oysters Palatine

This is a dish of baked oysters and spinach with curried hollandaise.

Ingredients

2 tablespoons unsalted butter
800g spinach, coarse stems discarded and leaves washed well and spun dry
20 oysters, shucked (reserving the bottom shells)
freshly ground white pepper to taste
For the curried hollandaise
300g unsalted butter
5 large egg yolks
2 tablespoons fresh lemon juice
2 tablespoons dry white wine
2 dashes of Tabasco sauce or to taste
1 teaspoon curry powder, or to taste

Method

1. In a large pan, melt the butter over moderately low heat, add the spinach and cook it, covered, stirring occasionally for 15 minutes, or until very tender. Drain in a colander. Squeeze out any excess liquid from the spinach, chop it, and season it with the white pepper and salt to taste. Let the chopped spinach cool completely.

2. To make the curried hollandaise, heat the butter in a small saucepan over a moderate heat until it is melted and foamy, but do not let it brown.

3. In a blender put yolks, lemon juice, wine, a pinch of salt, and Tabasco and turn machine on and immediately off. With the machine at low speed, add the melted butter in a stream. Cover the blender, increase the speed to high and blend the mixture for 1 minute. Add curry powder and blend the hollandaise well.

4. Arrange the reserved oyster shells on a large baking sheet, put an oyster in each shell, and top each one with about 1 tablespoon of spinach. Bake the oysters in the middle of a preheated 230oC oven for 10 minutes or until heated through. Top each oyster with 1 tablespoon of the curried hollandaise and place the oysters under a preheated grill about 10cm from the heat for 1 minute, or until the tops are browned lightly.

OYSTERS WITH PINK BUTTER

Ingredients

12 oysters in the shell
1 tablespoon minced shallots
9 tablespoons cold unsalted butter
1 tablespoon red wine vinegar
5 tablespoons red wine
Coarse Maldon salt and freshly ground black pepper, to taste
1 bunch of fresh chives, cut into 5mm lengths

Method

1. Prepare a grill or preheat the oven to very hot.

2. Place the oysters under the hot grill or on a baking sheet in the oven until they just begin to open. Open completely with a knife and remove the top shell.

3. While the oysters are opening, sauté the shallots in 1 tablespoon of the butter for about 30 seconds. Add the vinegar and wine and reduce the liquid by two thirds. Remove from the heat and whisk small pieces of the remaining cold butter into the remaining liquid, one piece at a time, until all is incorporated and the mixture is creamy. Add salt, pepper, and chives and spoon over the warm oysters.

OYSTER TARTS

Oysters are delicious luxury morsels of food, so please do not ruin them by overcooking – they only need warming. You can buy the little pastry cases used in this recipe readymade or make your own.

Ingredients

Oyster sauce (only buy the best and from a good oriental shop if possible)
Worcestershire sauce
anchovy sauce (optional)
30 oysters
30 pastry cases (you can buy these readymade to save time)

Method

1. To make the sauce, add Worcestershire sauce to oyster sauce to taste and add a dash of anchovy sauce if desired. Add oysters.

2. Spoon the mixture into the cases, making sure that each one contains one oyster. Then warm in a moderate oven for 10 minutes.

3. To serve, arrange attractively on a serving dish.

OYSTER SOUP

Top marks for this soup. It's a very old recipe and full of the good things needed for a delicious, nourishing soup. It's work, but worth the effort for all the praise you'll receive.

Ingredients

1kg fish bones for stock
3 cups milk
2 cups fish stock or water
1 carrot, sliced
1 small brown onion, chopped
2 bay leaves
pinch basil
4 peppercorns
salt
60g butter
1 tablespoon flour
2 egg yolks, beaten
1 cup cream
2 dozen oysters on the shell or bottled
few drops tabasco sauce
1 teaspoon Worcestershire sauce
finely chopped parsley

Method

1. Cut the fish bones into small pieces; put them in a saucepan with the milk, water, carrot, onion, bay leaves, basil, peppercorns and salt. Simmer gently for ½ hour.

2. Strain. Discard the bones, vegetables and seasonings.

3. Melt the butter in a pan, stir in the flour, add the strained fish stock, stir until boiling and cook for 3–5 minutes.

4. Beat the egg yolks and cream together, strain into the soup and stir for a few minutes, taking care that the soup does not boil. Carefully place the oysters in the soup, add tabasco sauce and Worcestershire sauce.

5. Garnish with parsley and serve with fried croutons, if you like, and serve immediately, so that the oysters are just warmed through.

Oysters Kilpatrick

Oysters Kilpatrick are very tasty served with a bowl of hot puréed spinach and thin slices of buttered brown or rye bread.

Ingredients

24 oysters on the shell
1 teaspoon Worcestershire sauce
1 cup cream
pepper and salt
250g smoked bacon rashers, chopped finely
fine breadcrumbs

Method

1. Remove the oysters from their shells and put them aside.

2. Place the shells on a baking sheet and heat in a moderate oven.

3. Mix the Worcestershire sauce and cream.

4. When the shells are hot, return the oysters to them. Use tongs to handle the shells, as they get very hot. Add a little of the cream mixture to each shell; sprinkle with pepper and salt.

5. Top each oyster with chopped bacon and fine breadcrumbs. Place the baking sheet under a hot grill and grill until the bacon is crisp but not burnt and the oysters are warmed through.

OYSTERS ROCKEFELLER

Ingredients

24 oysters on the shell
2 tablespoons butter
1 large clove garlic, crushed
3 stalks crisp celery, chopped finely
½ large red pepper or 1 small one, chopped finely
freshly ground pepper and salt
250g bacon, rind removed, chopped
pinch cayenne
1½ cups breadcrumbs or more as needed
1 teaspoon Worcestershire sauce
2 tablespoons cream

Method

1. Remove the oysters from their shells and put them aside.

2. Heat the shells under a grill.

3. Melt the butter in a heavy frying pan, being careful not to let it burn. Add garlic and twist around pan for a few seconds for flavour, then discard. Add celery, red pepper, freshly ground pepper and salt, and chopped bacon. Cook slowly until all is tender, 10–15 minutes. Add a pinch of cayenne.

4. Mix the breadcrumbs with Worcestershire sauce and cream. Put aside. Remove shells from under the hot grill, spoon a little celery, pepper and bacon mixture into each shell, then place the fresh oyster on top.

5. Top with bread mixture and grill under medium heat until bread mixture is browned and oysters are just warmed through. If you think the oysters need more breadcrumbs, just sprinkle extra over.

Oyster Mornay Superb

Rich, succulent oysters in a creamy white sauce. Who could ask for anything more?

Ingredients

2½ cups milk
1 small onion, finely chopped
freshly ground pepper
pinch salt
4 drops tabasco
pinch basil or dill
½ teaspoon celery salt
2 tablespoons plain flour
1 teaspoon mustard
1 tablespoon butter
1 large carrot, scraped and finely grated
2 tablespoons cream
24 oysters on the shell
tasty cheese, grated

Method

1. Put the milk to heat in a saucepan, add onion, pepper, salt, tabasco, basil and celery salt.

2. Mix the plain flour and mustard to a smooth paste with water. When the milk mixture is very hot, but not boiling, stir in the flour and mustard mixture. Add the butter, stir until all is combined and thickened. Cook slowly for 15 minutes, stirring occasionally to see that mixture does not stick and burn. When ready, stir in grated carrot; remove from the heat and stir in the cream.

3. Remove the oysters from their shells and add to the sauce. Return the pan to the heat to warm through, meanwhile heating shells under a hot grill. When all is ready, fill shells with oysters and sauce, sprinkle with grated cheese and put under the grill again, to brown. Superb!

DEVILLED OYSTERS

Ingredients

2 tablespoons butter
2 teaspoons curry powder, or to taste
1 tablespoon Worcestershire sauce
1 teaspoon anchovy sauce
small pinch cayenne
juice of 1 lemon
2 eggs, well beaten
1 cup milk
2 teaspoons cornflour
24 oysters, bottled or on the shell
paprika
lemon wedges

Method

1. Mix the butter, curry powder, Worcestershire sauce, anchovy sauce, that tiny pinch of cayenne and lemon juice in a bowl.

2. Add the beaten eggs and milk and mix well.

3. Pour the mixture into a saucepan. Cook slowly for 10 minutes, stirring, and then thicken with cornflour that has been mixed to a smooth paste with a little milk.

4. When the mixture has boiled and thickened, add the oysters.

5. Do not overcook the oysters; just cook for a few minutes to reheat and flavour.

6. Serve on a bed of fluffy rice, with a sprinkle of paprika and plenty of lemon wedges. If you like your oysters hotter just increase the quantity of curry powder.

Oyster and Brie Soup

Ingredients

225g unsalted butter
1 cup onion, chopped
½ teaspoon cayenne pepper
450g Brie cheese, cut into small wedges, skin off
6 cups cold water
36 shucked oysters, with liquor
¼ cup dry sherry
1 cup celery, chopped
½ teaspoon white pepper
½ cup plain flour
2 cups double cream
½ cup Champagne (or Prosecco)

Method

1. In a large soup pot, melt half of the butter. Add the celery, onions, white pepper and cayenne. Stir and cook over a low heat until the vegetables begin to soften.

2. Over a low heat in another pan, make a roux by melting the rest of the butter and adding the flour to make a base for thickening the soup. Cook for at least 2 minutes, stirring constantly, so the floury taste is eliminated.

3. Add the roux and the cheese to the soup pot. Add the water, cream, oysters and their liquid. Simmer the soup until the oysters begin to curl. Add the champagne and sherry and heat through.

GRILLED OYSTERS WITH MUSHROOMS AND SPARKLING WINE SAUCE

Ingredients

12 oysters
¼ pound oyster mushrooms, finely minced
2 tablespoons unsalted butter
For the sauce
2 shallots, very finely minced
1 cup sparkling white wine
1 tablespoon fresh lemon juice
2 egg yolks
¼ cup unsalted butter, cubed
¼ cup crème fraiche
salt and fresh ground white pepper

Method

1. Scrub the oyster shells under cold water, pat dry and shuck, reserving the liquid.

2. Fill an oven proof pan or container with 1cm of rock salt and place the oysters on the half shell on top of this.

3. Melt the butter in a frying pan, add the oyster mushrooms and cook until au sec (dry).

4. To make the sauce, combine ¾ cup sparkling wine, shallots, and lemon juice in a saucepan, reduce to about 1–2 tablespoons.

5. Lower the heat to the lowest possible and slowly whisk in the butter one cube at a time, the butter should be emulsified rather than just melted.

6. In a metal bowl combine egg yolks, remaining sparkling wine and reserved oyster juice; gently cook over a double boiler whisking until thick.

7. Remove the egg yolk mixture from the heat immediately and slowly whisk in the butter mixture, then whisk in ¼ cup crème fraiche and season to taste, and pass through a fine strainer.

8. Spoon ½ tablespoon of oyster mushrooms over each oyster followed by about 1 tablespoon sauce. Grill for about 3 minutes until brown, serve at once.

HUITRES AU CHAMPAGNE
(FRESH OYSTERS WITH CHAMPAGNE)

Ingredients

12 fresh oysters
1 shallot, minced
1 cup double cream
½ cup champagne (or Prosecco)
1 tablespoon unsalted butter

Method

1. Shuck the oysters, being careful to preserve the juice. Wash the shells and save, as the cooked oysters will be served in the original shells.

2. Place the oysters in a saucepan with the oyster juice and cook for 3 minutes. Remove the oysters and keep warm.

3. Add the cream, champagne and the minced shallot to the hot oyster juice. Cook over a medium heat until the sauce is reduced by one-third. Swirl in the butter. Taste and correct the seasoning if necessary.

4. Serve the oysters in the shells with a bit of the sauce in each one.

Note: You can garnish this dish with caviar to make it extra sumptuous. This dish is particularly delicious when served with the same champagne used in its preparation.

GRILLED OYSTERS WITH HERB CHEVRE AND PARMA HAM

Ingredients

12 oysters, shucked
150g soft chevre (goats cheese)
3 tablespoons mixed fresh herbs, finely chopped (chives, tarragon, dill, chervil)
freshly ground pepper
6 slices of Parma ham
12 sprigs of chervil

Method

1. Mix the chevre, herbs and pepper together until well combined.

2. Open the oysters, discarding the top shell, and pour off the juices. Place a generous teaspoonful of chevre on each oyster. Wrap the oyster and chevre in ½ slice of Parma, sealing in the cheese.

3. Preheat the grill on a high setting. Place the oysters on a baking tray and cook them under the grill for 3–5 minutes so that the oysters are just opaque and the Parma is not dry.

4. Place 6 oysters each on two plates and garnish each one with chervil springs. Serve hot.

CAESAR SALAD WITH FRIED OYSTERS

Ingredients

For the salad

1 head Romaine lettuce
½ head iceberg lettuce
good olive oil (to taste really, I like lots so I would add at least
half a cup)
1 clove minced garlic
1 teaspoon Dijon mustard
juice from one lemon
1 egg yolk
½ cup grated Parmigiano cheese
2 cups croutons (home made is best)
anchovies

For the fried oysters

36 oysters
3 tablespoons milk
2 eggs beaten
½ cup plain flour
½ cup dry breadcrumbs or cracker crumbs
½ teaspoon salt
¼ teaspoon pepper
oil for shallow frying

Method

1. Shuck the oysters and reserve them separately from the oyster
    liquor. Discard the shells.

2. Place the flour in a bowl. Place the eggs in another bowl and whisk with 3 tablespoons of milk. Place the bread crumbs in a third bowl. Season the flour and bread crumbs with salt and pepper. Dredge the oysters in the flour first and tap off the excess. Next dip them in the egg mixture and then in the breadcrumbs.

3. In a small saucepan heat 2.5cm of oil to 190°C.

4. For the dressing, in a bowl, whisk together the reserved oyster liquor, the garlic, mustard, lemon juice, mashed anchovies and egg yolk until well blended. Add the olive oil slowly in a steady stream and whisk until smooth. Season to taste with salt and pepper.

5. Deep fry the oysters, a few at a time, until golden, 1 minute. Remove with a slotted spoon and drain on paper towels.

6. Place the lettuce in a large bowl and toss with the dressing until the leaves are coated. Add half of the Parmigiano and toss again. Place on serving plates, top each plate with 3 oysters and sprinkle with the remaining Parmigiano. Serve immediately.

OYSTERS MOMBASA

Whether or not the Swahili and other African peoples of the Eastern African coast traditionally ate oysters does not seem to be well documented. There are very few recipes for oysters in African cookbooks, and those that there are come from Western Africa. Thus, it seems possible that Oysters Mombasa originated among expatriates in Africa during the era of British colonialism in Kenya. Mombasa, an island-port city on the Indian ocean, served as the gateway to the 'white highlands' and 'Happy Valley' of Kenya for European settlers arriving by ship. It's easy to imagine jazz-age European elites eating oysters like this in Mombasa's hotels and restaurants. To this day, Kenyan oysters are featured on the menus of restaurants and resorts, mostly frequented by tourists, along the Kenyan coast.

Ingredients

½ cup butter
3 cloves garlic, finely minced
1 small bunch of parsley chopped
Tabasco (or similar) sauce, to taste
½ cup white wine
salt, black pepper, and red pepper; to taste
two to three dozen fresh oysters, cleaned and left on the half shell

Method

1. Preheat the oven to 180°C.

2. To prepare the sauce: melt the butter in a saucepan. Add garlic and parsley (or cilantro). Sauté for a few minutes. Add hot sauce, wine, salt, and pepper. Remove from the heat.

3. Arrange the oysters on a baking sheet. Drizzle a spoonful of sauce over each oyster.

4. Bake the oysters for 6–8 minutes. Serve immediately with lemon wedges and the remaining sauce or additional hot sauce on the side.

BARBECUED OYSTERS

Take care with this one. Bram Haward of the famous Haward oyster fisheries and I tried this and one of the oysters exploded. Hence the aluminum foil. It whizzed past Bram's ear and a number of fisherman's salty expressions formed on Bram's lips. So gently with this one on not too hot coals and with a good distance from the heat.

Method

1. Prepare the barbecue or grill. Place the oysters on the ungreased barbecue or grill at least 10cm from the hot coals or heat element. Be sure the oysters are rounded side down so they cook in their own juices.

2. Loosely cover oysters with a tent of aluminum foil.

3. Cook for 7–10 minutes, depending on the size of the oysters.

4. Do not turn the oysters during cooking. Shells may open slightly when the oysters are done, but not always. Look for steam or bubbles around the fluted edges as a signal that they are ready. If they have not fully opened take care when opening them as the liquid inside can be very hot.

LAST WORD

Cooking oysters has been popular through the ages. Indeed the great British steak and kidney pud in Victorian times often had oysters added. Cooking oysters is still very common in Asia and the USA but in Europe it is going through a temporary lull.

Let's be cutting edge and ahead of fashion. Let's get stuck in, enjoy and fall in love with cooked oysters once more.

Generally speaking the rock (gigas/pacific) oysters are plentiful, not too expensive and perfect for cooking, so stick to them.

Getting cooked oysters in restaurants in the UK is not easy but most of the recipes in this book you have just read are practical and in many cases very easy. Above all they are tasty, healthy and do not have the risks, small though they are, of eating raw oysters.

Don Quinn

ACKNOWLEDGEMENTS

Thanks to Cath and Sue. To Simon Avery a lovely man who designed the cover. My wonderful son in law Demi who helped lots and refrained from getting too cross with me. To Steve Green of Green Square, a great bloke. And Simon Pitham of AutoPrint. Not just a superb printer but also a mate.

Above all to Jean, my wife, who hates bloody oysters, and frequently had to clear up the kitchen mess after my experiments.

This book is dedicated to my granddaughters
Lexi, Laya and Natalie
with love from grandad